SEVERE WEATHER

DUST STORMS

BY MEGAN GENDELL

WWW.APEXEDITIONS.COM

Apex is distributed by North Star Editions:
sales@northstareditions.com | 888-417-0195

Produced for Apex by Red Line Editorial.

Photographs ©: Shutterstock Images, cover, 1, 4–5, 6–7, 8, 9, 12–13, 14–15, 16–17, 18–19, 24–25, 29; iStockphoto, 10–11, 13, 22–23, 26–27; Hadi Mizban/AP Images, 21; Peter Adams/Jon Arnold Images Ltd/Alamy, 27

Library of Congress Control Number: 2022901431

ISBN
978-1-63738-302-5 (hardcover)
978-1-63738-338-4 (paperback)
978-1-63738-407-7 (ebook pdf)
978-1-63738-374-2 (hosted ebook)

Printed in the United States of America
Mankato, MN
082022

NOTE TO PARENTS AND EDUCATORS

Apex books are designed to build literacy skills in striving readers. Exciting, high-interest content attracts and holds readers' attention. The text is carefully leveled to allow students to achieve success quickly. Additional features, such as bolded glossary words for difficult terms, help build comprehension.

TABLE OF CONTENTS

CHAPTER 1
DUST IN THE WIND 4

CHAPTER 2
FORMING A STORM 10

CHAPTER 3
DANGEROUS DUST 16

CHAPTER 4
CLEARING THE AIR 22

COMPREHENSION QUESTIONS • 28
GLOSSARY • 30
TO LEARN MORE • 31
ABOUT THE AUTHOR • 31
INDEX • 32

CHAPTER 1

DUST IN THE WIND

It's a hot, dry afternoon in the desert. A large thunderstorm is forming. Big clouds rise overhead. But it is not raining yet.

Most dust storms are caused by wind from thunderstorms.

Strong winds rush across the land. They pick up loose dirt from the ground. Dust blows into the air.

A dust storm can reach thousands of feet into the air.

FAST FACT

Dust storm winds can blow up to 70 miles per hour (113 km/h).

It can be very difficult to see anything during a dust storm.

Soon, a wall of dust blocks the sun. People can hardly see. Half an hour later, the wind dies down. The dust storm is over.

Dust storms fling lots of dust all over. It even gets inside people's homes.

DESERT DUST

A haboob is a dust storm or sandstorm with strong winds. Haboobs can happen near the Sahara Desert in northern Africa. They can also happen in Arizona and India. The storms can be miles long.

CHAPTER 2

FORMING A STORM

Dust storms begin with strong winds. They are common in dry places. Dry soil and dust blow away easily.

Most dust storms happen during the spring and summer.

Dust storms often form over flat land or places without many trees. Wind can blow quickly in these places. Few things block it.

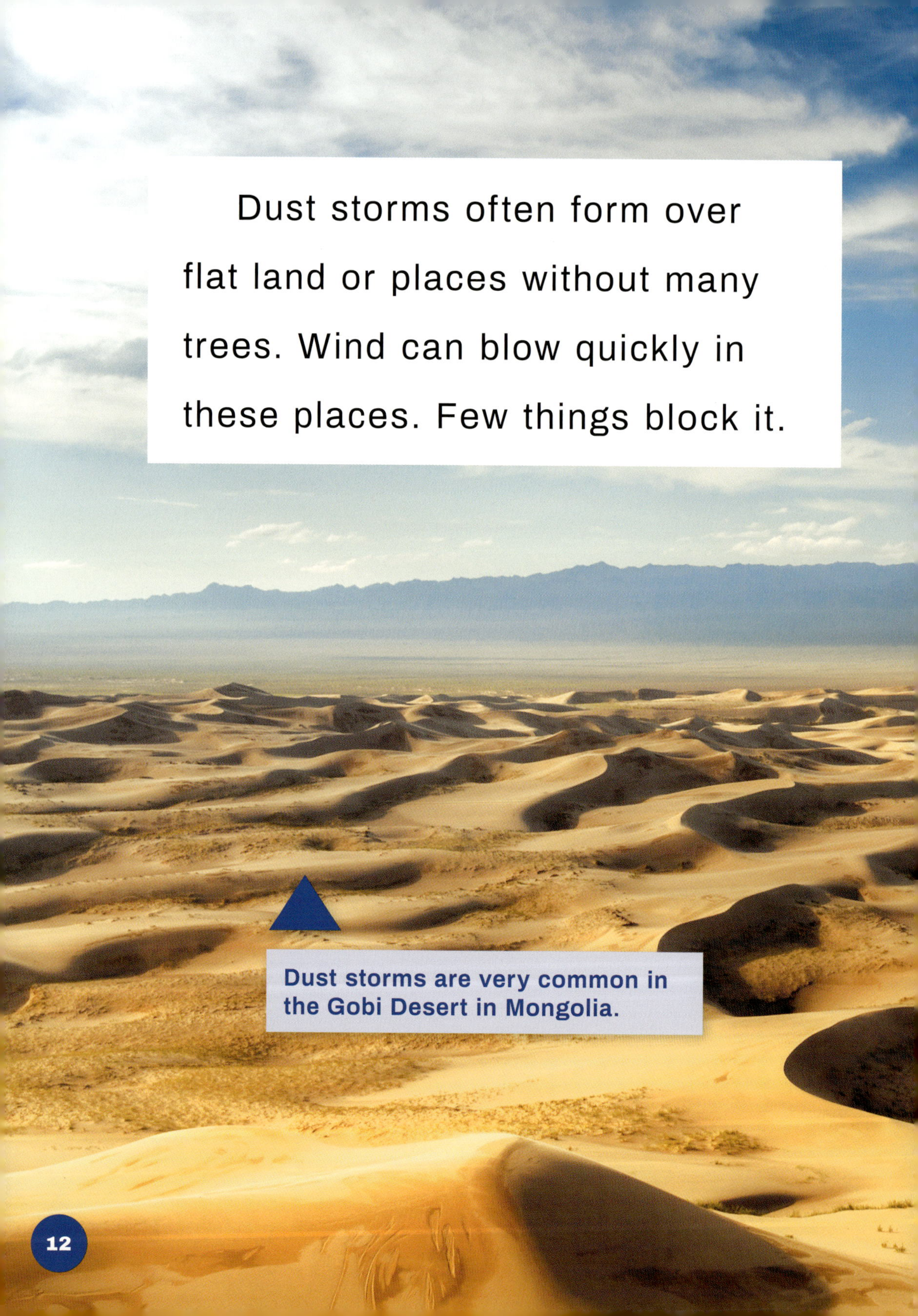

Dust storms are very common in the Gobi Desert in Mongolia.

Dust devils tend to happen in deserts or very dry areas.

FAST FACT

A dust devil is a whirlwind of sand or dust. It looks like a little tornado.

The wind creates a cloud of dust. This cloud can be miles wide. It moves quickly, too. The dust may travel thousands of miles.

The Sahara Desert has a lot of dust. Each year, enough blows away to fill more than 689,000 semitrucks.

Dust Journey

Dust from the Sahara Desert can blow across oceans. Sometimes it lands in Brazil. The dust has nutrients that help plants in the rain forest grow.

CHAPTER 3

DANGEROUS DUST

In the 1930s, the middle of the United States was very dry. This area was called the Dust Bowl. Dust storms killed many **crops** there.

During the 1930s, so much dust blew in the Dust Bowl that it blocked out the sun.

Sand filled the air during the 2006 Beijing storm.

In 2006, the Gobi Desert had a huge sandstorm. Tons of sand fell on Beijing, China. The air was **polluted**. Many people went to the hospital. They had problems breathing.

FAST FACT

Dust storms also happen on Mars. People can use **telescopes** to see them.

Iraq had 122 dust storms in 2008. A bad **drought** dried the ground. The dust damaged crops. People struggled to grow food.

WARMER AND DRIER

Climate change can make dust storms worse. As Earth gets warmer, land dries out faster. Dust blows away more easily. Larger dust storms could happen.

Iraq was covered in dust for 283 days in 2008.

CHAPTER 4

CLEARING THE AIR

People are working to prevent dust storms. In some places, growing plants can help. Plants block the wind. Their roots also hold dirt in place.

People can plant trees in deserts to help make dust storms less likely.

Scientists keep watch for dust storms. They use **radar** and cameras. These tools help them track where a storm is heading. Scientists can warn people before it hits.

Some signs warn drivers of areas where dust storms are likely to take place.

DANGEROUS DRIVING

Driving during a dust storm or sandstorm can be very dangerous. Dust can cover the road. People can't see. This can cause accidents.

Warnings give people time to prepare. They can go indoors. That way, they won't breathe in dust. Breathing dust can make people sick.

FAST FACT

Some dust carries **bacteria**. It can spread diseases.

People should stay inside instead of trying to drive during a dust storm.

Wearing a face covering helps people avoid breathing in dust.

COMPREHENSION QUESTIONS

Write your answers on a separate piece of paper.

1. Write a few sentences describing how dust storms form.

2. Is the place where you live likely to have dust storms? Why or why not?

3. Where are dust storms most common?

- **A.** rain forests with many trees
- **B.** flat areas with few trees
- **C.** wet places with many thunderstorms

4. How could dust storms damage crops?

- **A.** The dust could bury and kill plants.
- **B.** The dust could make plants grow faster.
- **C.** The dust could cover roads.

5. What does **whirlwind** mean in this book?

A dust devil is a whirlwind of sand or dust. It looks like a little tornado.

A. water that spins or swirls
B. air that spins or swirls
C. ice that falls from the sky

6. What does **struggled** mean in this book?

The dust damaged crops. People struggled to grow food.

A. did something easily
B. did something faster than usual
C. had a hard time doing something

Answer key on page 32.

GLOSSARY

bacteria

Tiny living things that can make people sick.

climate change

A dangerous long-term change in Earth's temperature and weather patterns.

crops

Plants that people grow for food.

drought

A time of little or no rain.

nutrients

Substances that help something grow and be healthy.

polluted

Made dirty or unsafe.

radar

A system that uses radio waves to find the position or speed of something.

telescopes

Tools that help people see things that are far away.

TO LEARN MORE

BOOKS

Hamalainen, Karina. *Extreme Weather and Rising Seas*. New York: Scholastic, 2020.

Roesser, Marie. *The Dust Bowl*. New York: Gareth Stevens Publishing, 2020.

Wilkins, Veronica B. *Dust Bowl*. Minneapolis: Jump!, 2020.

ONLINE RESOURCES

Visit **www.apexeditions.com** to find links and resources related to this title.

ABOUT THE AUTHOR

Megan Gendell is a writer and editor. She lives in Vermont. She loves big thunderstorms.

INDEX

C

climate change, 20
clouds, 4, 14

D

dirt, 6, 22
dry, 4, 10, 16, 20
Dust Bowl, 16
dust devil, 13

G

Gobi Desert, 19

H

haboob, 9

I

Iraq, 20

M

Mars, 19

P

plants, 15, 22

R

radar, 24

S

Sahara Desert, 9, 15

W

warnings, 26
winds, 6–7, 8–9, 10, 12, 14, 22

ANSWER KEY:

1. Answers will vary; 2. Answers will vary; 3. B; 4. A; 5. B; 6. C